## ARE WE RECORDING?

RegularJOE here. First of all, the object you hold in your hands is dear to me, and I wanna thank you for buying it. Back when HITRECORD.ORG was a small, informal community of artists collaborating on a website that my brother, Dan and I made in our spare time, we liked to imagine pulling off projects on a grander scale, perhaps even breaking into mainstream media. Now, the better part of a decade later, it's happening. Our little community is making a television show: HITRECORD ON TV!

In the following pages, you'll find a few facts and figures describing how we made Season 1 of the show. Of course, the best way to see how we make things is just to come check out the site. Make something with us. Consider this your invitation. I do hope you enjoy these first eight episodes. But even more so, I hope you come work on the next ones.

## THANKS AGAIN <3
## J

# THE RECORD BREAK(DOWN)

ALL RECORDS FEATURED ON
SEASON 1 OF HITRECORD ON TV
BY RECORD TYPE OUT OF

## 54,980

TOTAL CONTRIBUTIONS

490

140

4,220
FEATURED

1,775

1,815

## REGULARITIES

**112**

LONGEST REGULARITY:
6:40 MINs

SHORTEST REGULARITY:
1:24 MINs

## REQUESTS VIDEOS

**173**

MOST frequent request made FOR:
**WRITERS**

LEAST frequent request made FOR:
francophiles

## COLLABORATIONS

**115**

TOTAL CONTRIBUTIONS:
**61,764**

COLLAB WITH THE MOST CONTRIBUTIONS:
4,311  PATTERNS

COLLAB WITH THE LEAST CONTRIBUTIONS:
12  GAMES COLD OPEN

AVERAGE CONTRIBUTIONS PER COLLAB:
**537.07**

SHORTEST LENGTH OF A COLLAB FROM START TO FINISH:
24 DAYS  BEASTLY BEAUTY

LONGEST LENGTH OF A COLLAB FROM START TO FINISH:
181 DAYS  CAPTURE THE FLAG

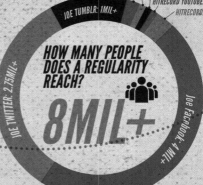

JOE YOUTUBE: 165k+
HITRECORD facebook: 53k+
**HITRECORD TWITTER: 53k+**
HITRECORD YOUTUBE: 89k+
HITRECORD: 325k+

JOE TUMBLR: 1MIL+

JOE TWITTER: 2.75MIL+

Joe Facebook: 4MIL+

### HOW MANY PEOPLE DOES A REGULARITY REACH?

## 8MIL+

---

## 22 REGULARITIES WERE FILMED OUTSIDE THE HITRECORD OFFICE:

| 2 | 1 | 1 | 5 | 1 | 1 | 1 | 1 | 9 |
|---|---|---|---|---|---|---|---|---|
|  |  |  |  |  |  |  |  |  |
| ELEVATOR | REC ROOM | DANCE STUDIO | CAR | DRESSING ROOM | AIRPORT | BORDER | FILM FESTIVAL | HOTEL ROOM |

DAYS OF PRODUCTION

# PRODUCTION TIMEFRAME:

# 235

DAYS OF PRE-PRODUCTION WITHOUT WORKING INTERNET AT OFFICE

**JUN 10** ▧▧▧▧▧▧▧▧▧▧ **JAN 31**

7 MONTHS, 2 WEEKS, 6 DAYS

# 1,295
## CONTRIBUTING ARTISTS

**707** — CONTRIBUTORS WITH A SINGLE RECORD FEATURED

**3 $\frac{1}{4}$** — AVERAGE NUMBER OF RECORDS PER CONTRIBUTING ARTIST

**90** — MOST RECORDS BY A SINGLE ARTIST: PONYTAILSANDCAPRIS

RE: AMERICA

RE: INDEPENDENCE

RE: THE ROAD

RE: FAKING

To
C

RE: THE #1

RE: FANTASY

RE: TRASH

RE: SPA

TRASH

SPACE

RE: MAGIC

RE: THE BIBLE

RE: MY FAVORITE THINGS

RE: SECRETS

RE: PATTERNS

RE: MONEY

Strangest theme
*CANNIBALISM*

RE: GAMES

RE: THE OTHER SIDE

emes
uted
7

# ANATOMY OF A RECORD:
# MAKING "FIRST STARS I SEE TONIGHT"

TOTAL COUNTRIES
## 13

COUNTRIES OF ORIGIN FOR EACH ARTIST WITH A RECORD FEATURED IN FIRST STARS I SEE TONIGHT

| | |
|---|---|
| 41 | UNITED STATES |
| 9 | UNITED KINGDOM |
| 3 | CANADA |
| 2 | AUSTRALIA |
| 2 | FRANCE |
| 2 | GERMANY |
| 1 | BELGIUM |
| 1 | CYPRUS |
| 1 | DENMARK |
| 1 | IRELAND |
| 1 | NEW ZEALAND |
| 1 | PHILIPPINES |
| 1 | SLOVAKIA |

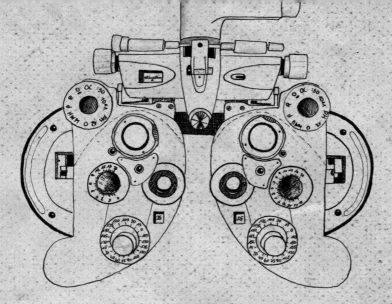

INITIAL CONCEPT COLLABORATION

1

E STARS WERE STOLEN

143

Total contributions
576

275

109

49

REQUEST VIDEOS

5
Request videos

(6/12/13) Writers and Visual Artists
(6/19/13) Female VO Request
(7/12/13) Story Boards
(7/17/13) Visuals #1
(8/14/13) Visuals #2

FINAL FILM

12

TOTAL
CONTRIBUTORS
66

45

4

5

FIRST STARS I SEE TONIGHT

REQUEST VIDEOS

2
Request videos

(9/10/13) Musicians
(9/24/13) Actors

REQUEST VIDEOS

E STARS I SEE TONIGHT

2

81

Total contributions
864

685

6

95

Audio    Image    Video    Text

FINAL PRODUCTION COLLABORATION

# SHOOTING ON LOCATION
# LIVE SHOWS

Trash Monologue

The Number One Monologue

Patterns Monologue

Money Monologue

Capture th

The Number One Monologue

Patterns Monologue

The Number One Monologue

Fantasy Monologue

Space Monologue

Fantasy Monologue

Front Lawn Freak

Trash Mates

You're Not the Only One

Space Monologue

The Other Side Monologue

Above It All

Space X

Games Monologue

We Can Go Back Again

The Money Tree

Money Monologue

Adieu

The Universe Tiny Story

Patterns Monologue

We Can Go Back Again

Oh, It's Fantastic!

Weep for the King

SAN DIEGO/TIJUANA BORDER

CHECKS CASHED

PIERCE COLLEGE FIL

SPACE X HQ

KGS BAKER MARIONETTE

Tournament of Champions

744 contributions

830 contributions

The Never-Wrongs and the Ever-Rights

300 people

First Kiss

200 people

We Can Go Back Again

**THE TROUBADOUR**
SAT • AUG 10TH 2013• 8PM

**MASONIC LODGE**
SUN • JUN 30TH 2013 • 8PM

**98** DEGREES
Hottest Indoor Show (Literally)

**1** PAIR OF SUIT PANTS
Ripped During Death Scene

**ORPHEUM THEATRE**
SAT • AUG 10TH 2013 • 8PM

**4.5** HOURS
Longest Live Show

1,800 people

2,684 contributions

FEATURING **1,295** CONTRIBUTORS FROM **54,980** CONTRIBUTIONS

## HITRECORD *is*

**Joseph Gordon-Levitt,** *Director*
**Jared Geller,** *Producer*
**Marke Johnson,** *Creative Director*
**Vance Heron,** *Director of Engineering*
**Chris Jacobs,** *General Manager*
**Abigail Lake,** *Controller*
**Matt Conley,** *Community Director*
**Gregory Abraham,** *Editor*
**Rebecca Votta,** *Assistant Editor*
**Adam Blake,** *Project Designer*
**Brian Bonus,** *Front End Developer*
**Jeff Sudakin,** *Audio Supervisor*
**Keir Schmidt,** *Music Coordinator*
**Jen Gerdano,** *Intern*
*and*
**A worldwide community of 317,147 artists** *as of June 17, 2014*

**DEY ST.**

Printed in China.

HarperCollins books may be purchased for educational, business, or sales
promotional use. For information, please e-mail the Special Markets Department at
SPsales@harpercollins.com.

FIRST EDITION

Library of Congress Cataloging-in-Publication Data has been applied for.

ISBN: 978-0-06-237203-1

14  15  16  17  18    OV/RRD    10  9  8  7  6  5  4  3  2  1

# RE:
# THE NUMBER

HITRECORD on TV **RE: THE NUMBER ONE**

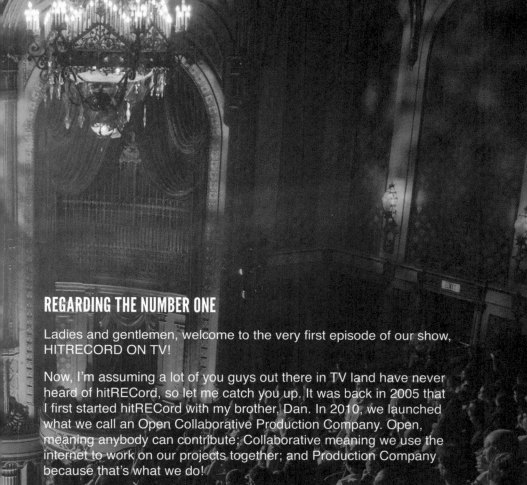

## REGARDING THE NUMBER ONE

Ladies and gentlemen, welcome to the very first episode of our show, HITRECORD ON TV!

Now, I'm assuming a lot of you guys out there in TV land have never heard of hitRECord, so let me catch you up. It was back in 2005 that I first started hitRECord with my brother, Dan. In 2010, we launched what we call an Open Collaborative Production Company. Open, meaning anybody can contribute; Collaborative meaning we use the internet to work on our projects together; and Production Company because that's what we do!

We've screened our short films at Sundance and other festivals, we've published books, we've put out records, we've gone out on tour. But it's all been leading up to this.

Now, we get to hit RECord on TV.

Everything you're going to see on this show has been made collaboratively by a community of hundreds of thousands of artists from all over the world. And each episode is going to be revolving around a different theme.

So, I figured, since this is our first-ever episode, it will be

NUMERO UNO. THE CHAMPION. THE GUINEA PIG.
PULLING ON A ONE-ARMED BANDIT
WITH A ONE-IN-A-MILLION SHOT AT GETTING OUT OF THIS ONE-HORSE TOWN.

THEY SAY ONE IS THE LONELIEST NUMBER,
BUT THIS ONE CONTRIBUTOR ON THE SITE WHO GOES BY J-BELT, HE WROTE "ANYBODY WHO THINKS THAT ONE IS
THE LONELIEST NUMBER HAS NEVER HAD TO BE THE THIRD WHEEL." HE SAID "THREE IS THE LONELIEST NUMBER,
ONE IS GREAT, TWO IS COMPANY, THREE SUCKS."

THE NUMBER ONE CAN MEAN UNITY,
LIKE ALL FOR ONE
AND ONE FOR ALL

AND YOU CAN ASK A TAOIST MONK, OR A QUANTUM PHYSICIST, THEY'LL TELL YOU THE SAME THING.
EVERYBODY AND EVERYTHING EVERYWHERE IS ALL ONE

WE'RE NUMBER 1!

THE NUMBER ONE ALSO MAKES YOU THINK OF YOUR FIRST TIME.
THERE'S A FIRST TIME FOR EVERYTHING, AND YOU NEVER GET A SECOND CHANCE TO MAKE A FIRST IMPRESSION.
DO YOU REMEMBER YOUR FIRST TIME?
AND I MEAN, YOUR FIRST TIME DOING ANYTHING.

# FIRST STARS
# I SEE TONIGHT

FEATURING   12   75   5   13   RECORDS
VIDEO  IMAGE  TEXT  AUDIO

FROM 1,440 CONTRIBUTIONS

**roswellgray**
WRITER   Ⓣ   Lincoln, Nebraska

*I can now say that I've dropped the F-bomb to a national television audience, and the world can see how cool my dad really is.*

# ONE

It was not the panic of greed that sent adrenaline coursing through me, but rather, a horrifying sense that my selection of only one meant the rejection of everything else.

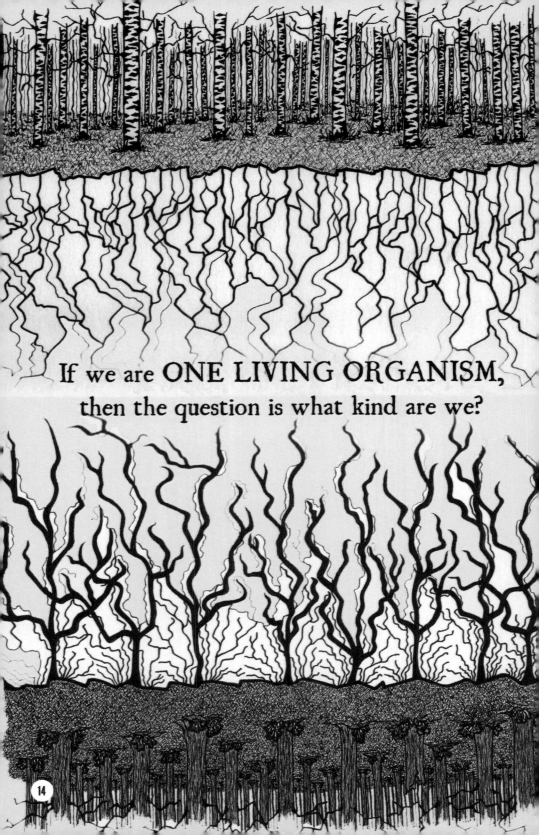

If we are ONE LIVING ORGANISM,
then the question is what kind are we?

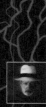

## Saintmaker

CONCEPT ⓣ Bastrop, Texas

Joe announced that Davis Guggenheim would be directing the "One Living Organism" segment about the Pando Forest in Utah. It seemed to be such a feel-good story: one giant living organism living in harmony with nature. So, naturally, I felt the need to find a dark side to this story. And I did: the honey mushroom in Malheur National Forest in Oregon, an even larger living organism that kills everything around it.

There are usually at least two sides to every story...including at least one dark side. Somewhere along the line, it has become my lot in life to find it. Hey, somebody has to.

FEATURING   58        6        3        7    RECORDS

VIDEO   IMAGE   TEXT   AUDIO

FROM 506 CONTRIBUTIONS

THE PRINCESSES

THE TROLLS

THE ENGINEERS

THE GLOOMS

 **wirrow**

**WRITER & RESIDENT DIRECTOR OF ANIMATIONS** (t) London, England

WHEN I WAS A KID MY DREAM WAS TO WORK ON A CARTOON FOR TV. AND SO BASICALLY, THAT DREAM CAME TRUE WITH THIS PROJECT! I LOOK FORWARD TO HITRECORD ON TV FULFILLING MORE OF MY CHILDHOOD DREAMS. WILL THEY SEND ME TO SPACE? WHO KNOWS. THE SHOW IS STILL YOUNG. I'M PATIENT.

# ONE + SONG

PRINCESSES

WE'LL USE OUR SWEET, PREDICTABLE PATTERNS TO LURE HIM,
AND MAKE HIM FEEL ALL SAFE AND SECURE, THEN:

ENGINEERS

OUR HIGH TECH LASERS WILL SHOOT AT HIS HEAD,
TO DAZE HIM, CONFUSE HIM, AND FILL HIM WITH DREAD;

GLOOMS

NOW THAT HE'S ANGSTY AND CONFUSED,
OUR SOMBER CLOUD WILL DEPRESS HIS MOOD;

TROLLS

THEN, OUR MOSH MONSTER WILL TAKE THE STAGE,
FEEL HIS FIERY FISTS OF RAGE!

FEATURING    1 VIDEO    3 IMAGE    2 TEXT    18 AUDIO    RECORDS

FROM 564 CONTRIBUTIONS

Our first kiss...
The most romantic moment you could imagine. I turned to him and went for it.

I missed.

## DianeFT
**VIDEO CONTRIBUTOR** ▶ Ottawa, Canada

I asked my son what he thought of when he heard the theme "number one,"
and the first thing that popped into his head and out of his mouth was "pee."

I will **NOT** be interviewing him for the theme "number two."

# YOU'RE NOT THE ONLY ONE

featuring **66** video  **1** image  **1** text  **79** audio  records

from **934** contributions

## Samantha Vasquez
**VIDEO CONTRIBUTOR** San Diego, California

I usually only sing in the car or in the shower. I wasn't going to record myself singing "You're Not the Only One" chorus, until I saw Community Director Matt Conley sing. He did great, but I could see he was a bit nervous, which further pushed me to do it! It was fun to do something exciting and new!

Here I sing out loud
Is there anyone there?
I don't hear a sound I guess nobody dares
So I sing a bit louder than I did before
Still no ring on my phone, no knock on my door

And just as I
Had closed my eyes
And could no longer see
You sing to me...
"You're not the only one"

When I speak my mind
Did I say the right words?
Are they twisted signs?
Did I mean what you heard?
Listen close,
let me know that you know what it's like
Cause I'm telling the truth,
but I'm not sure it's right

Can you end the doubt
That what's without's
The same as what's within
And tell me again...
"You're not the only one"

And if all alone
Is all you are
The same thing goes for me
So listen and see that...
You're not the only one

# REGARDING
# THE OTHER SIDE

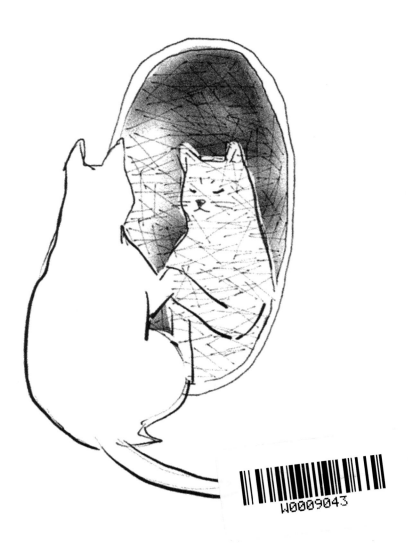

W0009043

HITRECORD on TV RE: THE OTHER SIDE

# SO, WHICH SIDE ARE YOU ON?

## RIGHT OR LEFT? RED OR BLUE? DEAD OR ALIVE?

ONE ARTIST ON THE SITE WROTE: "WHEN MY GRANDMOTHER DIED, ALL MY GRANDFATHER SAID WAS

## 'NOW SHE KNOWS THE BIG SECRET.'"

ME, I'M ALWAYS FASCINATED TO HEAR WHAT PEOPLE THINK HAPPENS WHEN WE DIE.

## DO WE BREAK ON THROUGH TO THE OTHER SIDE?

OR IS IT THAT THIS IS THE OTHER SIDE, AND ONCE WE COMPLETE OUR HERO'S JOURNEY,

# WE GET TO GO HOME?

THERE'S ANOTHER ARTIST ON THE SITE, SHE GOES BY BEAUTIFULDREAMER, AND SHE SAID,

# "I KNOW WHAT IT'S LIKE TO LIVE ON THE OTHER SIDE OF THINGS. I MOVED TO THE UNITED STATES FROM GUATEMALA WHEN I WAS SIX YEARS OLD."

I'M ALSO INTERESTED IN THE OTHER SIDE AS IT APPLIES TO MEDIA. BECAUSE RIGHT NOW, AS YOU'RE WATCHING ME SAY THIS, THERE'S SOME KIND OF SCREEN BETWEEN US. YOU'RE ON ONE SIDE AND I'M ON THE OTHER SIDE. THEN, OF COURSE, THERE'S THE

# OTHER SIDE OF THE STORY.

## EVERY STORY HAS MORE THAN ONE SIDE TO IT. EVERY MESSAGE CAN BE RECEIVED IN MORE THAN ONE WAY.

THE OTHER SIDE

### KaliBali

**VIDEO CONTRIBUTOR**  Inglewood, California

I wanted to share about my experience with racial profiling because I wasn't seeing very many contributions taking the theme in this direction. The night it aired, my house was full of hitRECorders, and none of us saw it coming. The immediate reaction was cheering because I was on TV, then there was a hush once everyone realized the topic of my testimonial. The feeling in the air was "shit just got real."

# The Other Side — Cold Open

A young child walks to a big wall. It's tall, but not too tall it
couldn't be climbed. He has a backpack and climbing gear
so he looks like a real explorer. With confidence, the kid begins
to climb the wall, curious to see what is on the other side.
As he climbs, the wall appears never-ending. But he doesn't
give up and keeps climbing. As he climbs, he grows older and
older until, finally, he gets all the way to the top and he is an
old man. The wall is now much much taller and bigger than it
was when he started climbing, but he is now up in the sky.
From the perspective of the other side of the wall, we see his
head appear over the top. We're looking directly at his face, but
we can't see what he is seeing. He looks amazed and
dumbfounded by what he finds there.

"The Other Side" is written on the wall below his head.

*Cold Open concept by Tori and IvanaK.*

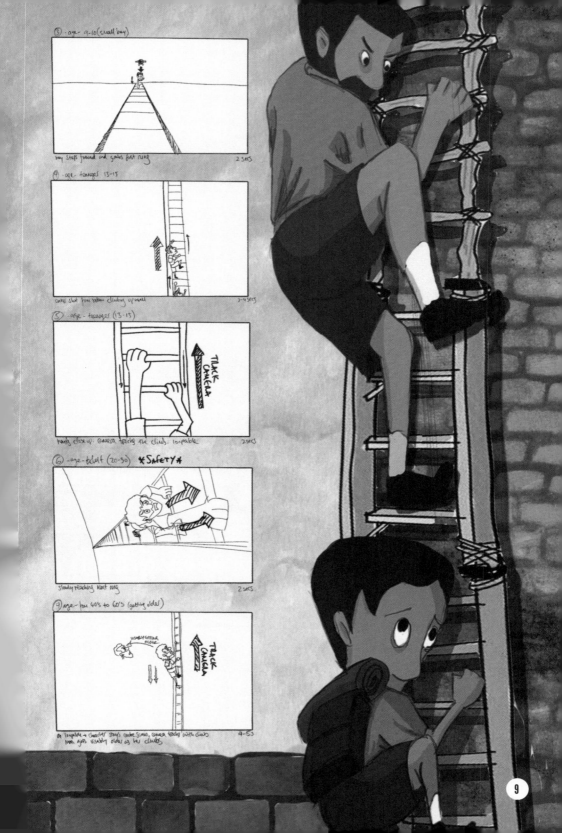

The thing about spending so much time
thinking about the other side of the story is
that you start forgetting which side you're on.

😊 is in the 👀 of the 🐝 holder

U 💩 🐤

Eat a 🌭

Whatever

The whole film takes place at 12:42 pm. Any place you see the time, on the Cat Clock or when Joe sends the text, I obviously had to make it 12:42.

FEATURING    ▶ **23**    📷 **137**    ⓣ **1**    ((●)) **4**    RECORDS

VIDEO    IMAGE    TEXT    AUDIO

FROM **518** CONTRIBUTIONS

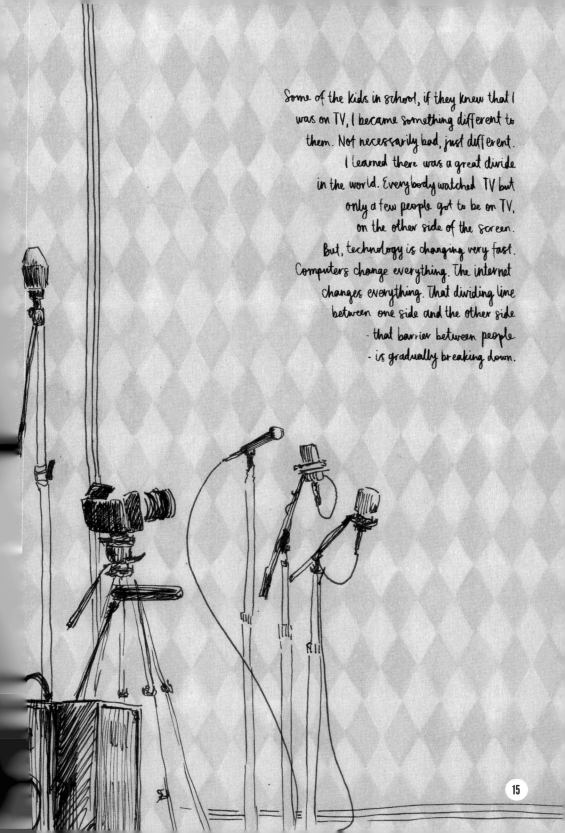

Some of the kids in school, if they knew that I was on TV, I became something different to them. Not necessarily bad, just different.
I learned there was a great divide in the world. Everybody watched TV but only a few people got to be on TV, on the other side of the screen.
But, technology is changing very fast. Computers change everything. The internet changes everything. That dividing line between one side and the other side
- that barrier between people
- is gradually breaking down.

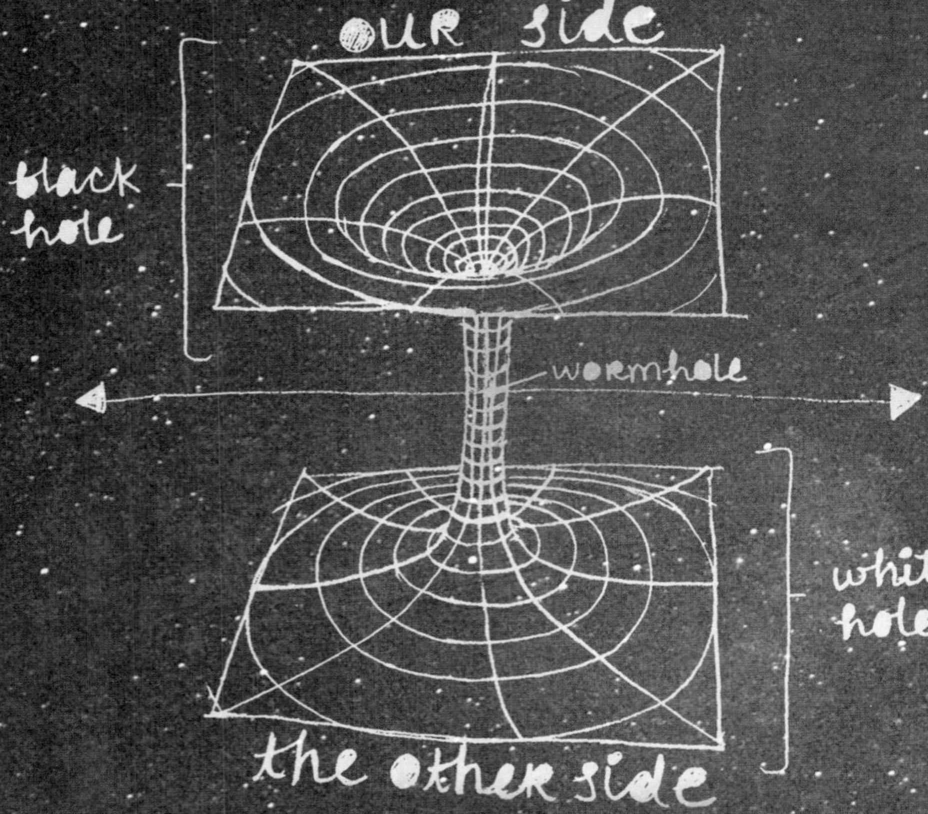

our side

black hole

wormhole

white hole

the other side

# Adieu

FEATURING  **15**  **1896**  **1**  **6**  RECORDS

VIDEO  IMAGE  TEXT  AUDIO

FROM **2,557** CONTRIBUTIONS

HITRECORD

## joerud

MUSIC & LYRICS ((o)) London, England

I never intended to write a song about death, especially one that would end up both sinister and comical. It was initially going to be a song about a man trying to recover a lover lost from unfaithful circumstances. But, as it turned out, I knew more French words about death than I did about love...

19

20